# I Wonder Why

# There's a Hole In The Sky

## and Other Questions About The Environment

### Sean Callery

**KINGFISHER**

First published 2008 by Kingfisher
an imprint of Macmillan Children's Books
a division of Macmillan Publishers Ltd
20 New Wharf Road
London N1 9RR
Basingstoke and Oxford
www.panmacmillan.com

Associated companies throughout the world

ISBN 978-0-7534-1704-1

9 8 7 6 5 4 3 2 1
1TR/0108/SHENS/RNBW(RNBW)/126.6MA/F

A CIP catalogue record for this book is available
from the British Library.

Printed in Taiwan

Illustrations: Mark Bergin 25, 30–31; Martin Camm
18–19; Peter Dennis (Linda Rogers Agency) 10, 12,
14–15, 26–27, 28; Chris Forsey cover, 16; Linden Artists 3,
9, 21, 22, 29; Julian Baker title page, 6, 8, 10–11, 30–31;
Peter Wilks (SGA) all cartoons.

# CONTENTS

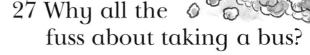
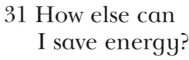

# Why is there life on Earth?

There is life on Earth because it is not too hot and not too cold. We are just the right distance from the Sun, which gives us heat and light. This is why there is no life on our neighbouring planets Venus (too hot) or Mars (too cold).

Sun

Mercury

Venus

Earth

Mars

Jupiter

- Some experts call Earth 'the Goldilocks planet' because, just like the porridge that Goldilocks eats in *Goldilocks and the Three Bears*, it is not too hot and not too cold.

# How can a star keep us warm?

The Sun is a star, just like the ones we see in the sky at night. It looks bigger than the other stars because it is much closer to us. The Sun's rays are very hot and they warm the Earth.

● It takes about eight minutes for the Sun's rays to reach Earth across space. They travel the 150 million kilometres at 1.8 billion kilometres an hour.

● Clouds are made of tiny drops of water. These bump into each other and make larger drops. When they get too big, they fall to the ground as rain or snow.

# Whatever is the weather?

There are all kinds of weather. It can be sunny, cloudy, wet, snowy, windy or stormy. Both the Sun's heat and changes in the air above Earth affect the weather. The usual weather of a region or country is called its climate.

**Some types of weather**

sunny

cloudy

heavy rain

thundery showers

snow

tropical storm

# Which blanket keeps the Earth warm?

The Earth is surrounded by the atmosphere, which is made up of gases. It reaches several hundred kilometres above the ground. The atmosphere has different layers (see right) and holds in heat like a blanket. It also helps to protect us from the Sun's rays.

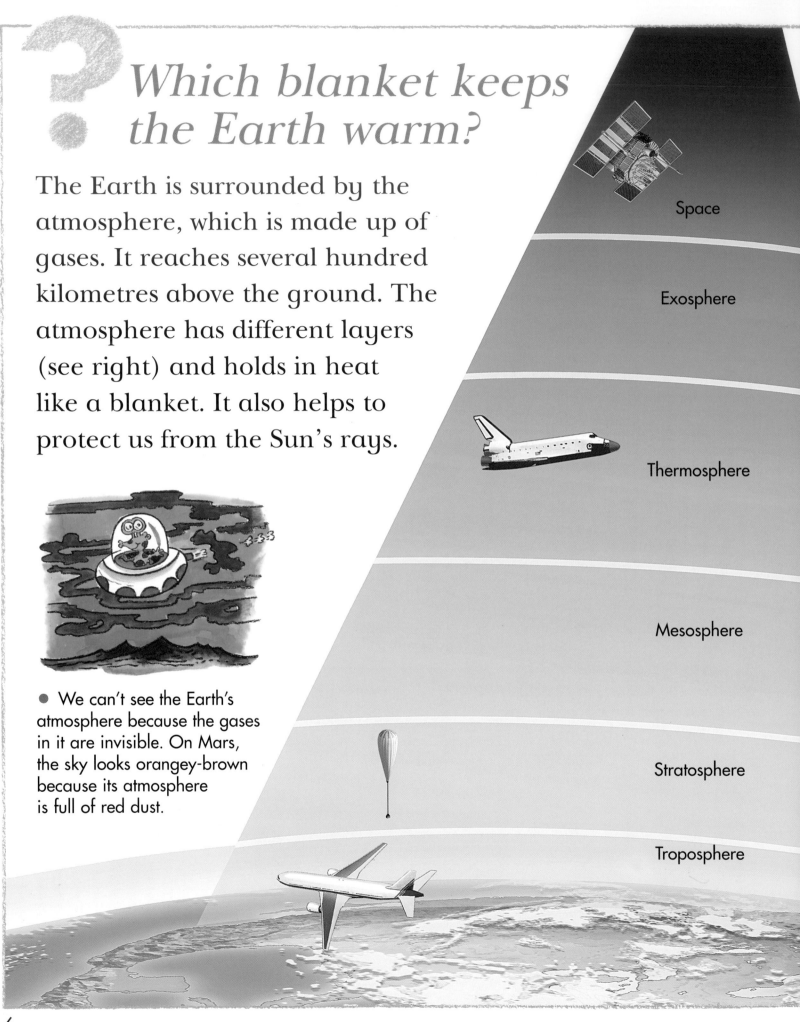

● We can't see the Earth's atmosphere because the gases in it are invisible. On Mars, the sky looks orangey-brown because its atmosphere is full of red dust.

Space

Exosphere

Thermosphere

Mesosphere

Stratosphere

Troposphere

# How is the atmosphere like a greenhouse?

Sun's heat

Some heat escapes

Heat is trapped

Earth

Sun

It gets very warm in a greenhouse as the glass walls and roof stop heat from escaping. Gases in our atmosphere trap heat in the same way and keep the Earth warm. They are called greenhouse gases.

● The atmosphere on Venus may once have been like ours, but surface temperatures are now about 460°C — much, much hotter than your oven at its hottest.

# What are greenhouse gases?

The main greenhouse gas is water vapour (water that has turned into a gas). Other greenhouse gases include carbon dioxide, methane and nitrous oxide (see pages 10–11). Some of these gases can remain in Earth's atmosphere for over 100 years.

● Greenhouse gases are made naturally and by the things people do. For example, both volcanoes and cars blast out carbon dioxide.

# Why are trees the bee's knees?

Trees take carbon dioxide from the air and they make oxygen, the gas we need to breathe. Trees also store carbon in their wood. If there were no trees, there would be so much carbon dioxide in the air that we wouldn't be able to breathe.

● Rainforests are home to two-thirds of all the different types of animals and plants on Earth. In fact, thousands of them are found only in rainforests.

# How does water cycle?

Water moves in a cycle. Tree roots soak up water. The water moves to the leaves and enters the air as vapour. This rises and turns into clouds. When it rains, the cycle starts again.

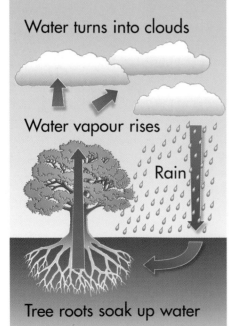

Water turns into clouds

Water vapour rises

Rain

Tree roots soak up water

● If you plant a tree, it will store carbon all its life. This will help cut greenhouse gases.

# Why can't we chop 'til we drop?

Cutting down and burning trees damages our planet. This is because there are fewer trees to make oxygen, and ground left behind is likely to flood. Also, burning wood releases carbon dioxide into the atmosphere.

● Over the last 60 years, about half the world's rainforests have been cut down. This is so people can use the wood and the land.

# What makes gas?

Carbon dioxide is given off by power stations burning coal, oil and gas. A lot of carbon dioxide also comes from vehicles such as cars, trucks and aeroplanes.

● Those pretty, wispy trails that aeroplanes leave behind in the sky are not good for the planet. They are made from water vapour and exhaust fumes containing carbon dioxide.

# Why is farming such a gas?

Some farmers put fertilizers that make nitrous oxide on their fields. Although there is not much of this gas in the atmosphere, it can hang around for 150 years. This is a problem because it traps heat.

# What's that smell?

When cows break wind they release methane gas, which goes up into the atmosphere. Many animals (including us) produce methane. This gas also comes from rotting rubbish and rice fields.

Rice farmers

● Cows make a lot of methane because they eat so much grass. This makes gas when it goes through their systems.

# Is it me or is it hot here?

All around the world, temperatures are rising. This is global warming. In the summer of 2003, Europe got so hot that 35,000 people died, and there were forest fires. The summer of 2005 broke high temperature records across the USA.

● The snow cap that has been at the top of Mount Kilimanjaro, in Africa, for 11,000 years is melting. By 2015, it may have gone completely.

# Is this a wind-up?

The world is seeing more extreme weather, such as hurricanes, tornadoes and typhoons. There are now twice as many big storms over the Atlantic Ocean as there were 100 years ago.

# Has our climate always changed?

The Earth has gone through several ice ages and different climates. For example, from 65 million years to 100 million years ago, the temperature was about 10°C warmer, and dinosaurs lived in forests at the South Pole. But the climate has never changed as fast as it is at the moment.

● Woolly mammoths lived in Siberia over 11,000 years ago. When temperatures rose by just a few degrees, it is possible that they couldn't stand the heat, and died out.

# Are we up to our necks in floods?

The world seems to be suffering more floods. Between 2005 and 2007, in Australia, the USA, India, the UK and eastern Europe, heavy rainfall caused landslides and made rivers burst their banks, flooding streets and houses.

● Scientists believe that five per cent more rain, snow and sleet is falling in the USA and Europe than 100 years ago.

# What's wrong with car parks?

Building roads and car parks makes floods more likely because water is unable to soak into the ground. Instead, it runs quickly off the top of the hard surfaces, causing problems.

● Lack of water is bad news, too. In 2007, there were major droughts in southern Europe. In Australia, a six-year-long drought, the worst on record, dried out rivers and caused water shortages.

# Who turned the rain off?

There have also been more droughts recently. In a drought, not enough rain falls. There is very little drinking water and it is difficult to grow crops. Since the 1970s, the number of serious droughts in the world has doubled.

# Why are poles hot stuff?

The Earth spins around the North and the South poles. The North Pole is in the Arctic and the South Pole is in the Antarctic. Both poles are covered in ice, but rising temperatures are making it melt. Even a small rise in temperature can melt huge amounts of polar ice.

● Soon there will not be enough sea ice in the Arctic for polar bears to live on. They are already losing weight as their hunting grounds disappear.

# Why is ice so cool?

As ice is white, it reflects the Sun's rays and helps to keep the Earth cool. Ice caps are an important habitat (home) for animals such as polar bears and penguins.

● If the entire Greenland ice sheet melted in the Arctic, sea levels would rise by seven metres. Countless coastal cities would be under water and entire low-lying countries, such as Bangladesh, would be destroyed.

# When is a river not a river?

Glaciers are rivers of ice that move very slowly. They drain into streams which supply water to people further down the river. Some glaciers are melting and getting smaller, so less water is reaching people.

● The total surface area of the world's glaciers has shrunk by half in the last 100 years.

# Why is there a hole in the sky?

High up in the atmosphere is the ozone layer. It filters out the Sun's harmful rays. The ozone layer is damaged by chemicals called chlorofluorocarbons (CFCs for short), which were used in spray cans and fridges. CFCs have made a big hole in the ozone layer over Antarctica.

Hole in the ozone layer

Antarctica

## Is the hole there the whole time?

No, the hole opens and closes with the seasons. The biggest hole so far appeared over Antarctica in 2006. There is no hole above the Arctic, but the ozone has got thinner. CFCs have been used less since 1987, and the damage to the ozone layer has slowed.

hydrochlorofluorocarbons

● CFCs have been replaced by hydrochlorofluorocarbons (or HCFCs) that are much less damaging, but even trickier to spell!

● Jet aeroplanes fly in the ozone layer, between 10 and 40 kilometres above the Earth's surface. Their engines release chemicals that damage the layer.

# How can water be bad for you?

We need fresh water to live, but when chemicals and human waste get into rivers and lakes, water becomes polluted (dirty). This kills five million people a year – that's about 14,000 deaths a day, just from dirty water.

# When is oil like glue?

When oil tankers leak, it causes huge damage to the environment, especially to seabirds, seals and sea otters. The oil sticks to their feathers or skin, and makes it hard for them to move or stay warm.

● In 1989, an oil tanker called *Exxon Valdez* spilled lots of oil in Alaska, killing between 250,000 and 500,000 seabirds, and 2,800 to 5,000 sea otters.

# What air makes you choke?

Smoke from factories, and fumes from engine exhaust pipes send dirt and gas into the air, making it hard to breathe. In some cities, you can see the pollution hanging in the air. This is called smog.

● In 1952, smog over London, UK, killed 12,000 people. The dense fog was called a 'pea souper' because it was thick, like pea soup.

# Why are some animals on the move?

Animals sense when the climate changes and, as a result, some are moving to cooler regions. In North America, the red fox is moving into the Arctic and threatening the Arctic fox, which cannot compete with its bigger cousin.

# Who needs a place to call home?

Elephants roam the grasslands of Africa and Asia. Much of this land is being turned into farmland, so the elephants are losing their habitat. This means that elephants could become extinct (die out).

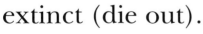

# Who is a tiger's worst enemy?

For a long time, people have hunted tigers for their skins and for their body parts, which are then used in medicines. Hunting tigers is now against the law in most countries, but people still catch them illegally.

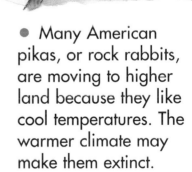

● Many American pikas, or rock rabbits, are moving to higher land because they like cool temperatures. The warmer climate may make them extinct.

● The dodo was a flightless bird that lived in Mauritius. It became extinct over 300 years ago when it was hunted to death.

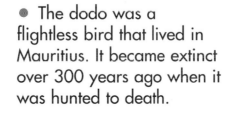

# What energy never runs out?

Energy from water, the wind or the Sun is called renewable energy. Unlike oil, gas or coal, it will never run out. Also, it does not produce carbon dioxide, so it will not speed up global warming.

● Scientists are trying to work out how to make power from the movement of waves. So, in the future, our homes could run on wave power.

# How can the Sun light up our nights?

Solar cells use the Sun's rays to make electricity. They can be used for lights in the garden, or in roof panels to power whole houses. Solar collectors use the Sun's heat to warm water.

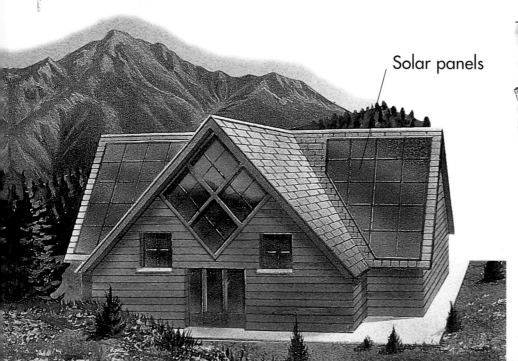

Solar panels

● If we covered the Sahara Desert with solar panels, it would make more electricity than the world could use.

# How is wind farmed?

People have used wind power for many years. The first wind-powered machines were windmills. Now, long blades spin at giant wind farms around the world. This type of farm can be built out at sea, too.

● Some power stations have started to burn crops such as straw, willow and elephant grass to make electricity.

# Why say 'bye to flying?

Aeroplanes give off a huge amount of carbon dioxide. To travel in a 'greener' way, take holidays closer to home instead of flying. If you have to fly, try to get a direct flight, because taking off and landing use the most energy.

# What are food miles?

If something you eat comes from another country, it travelled many 'food miles' to get to you, and lots of carbon dioxide was produced on the way. Buying food grown locally is often better for the environment.

# Why all the fuss about taking a bus?

Travelling by bus or train does less damage to the environment than going by car, because lots of people share the energy used.

● Cycling and walking are much better for the environment than using a car because they do not burn oil.

● If people share a car, they use less energy. Some roads have special lanes for cars carrying more than one person.

# Why is rubbish such a waste?

Most of our rubbish is burned, or buried in massive rubbish dumps called landfill sites. Rain can wash poisons from the rubbish through the soil and pollute the water supply. Landfill sites also release nasty gases into the air.

# What are the three Rs?

Reduce, Re-use and Recycle – we should reduce what we throw away, re-use things as much as possible, and when we don't need them any more, recycle rather than dumping them. As much as 70 per cent of our rubbish could be recycled.

● Recycling one aluminium can saves enough energy to run a television for three hours.

# When is a worm my friend?

Compost is a brilliant way to reduce waste and help the garden. Put old leaves, plants, fruit and vegetable peelings, eggshells and newspaper in a special bin outside. Worms and insects will turn it into soil for the garden.

● Cut-up newspaper is perfect in a compost bin because it soaks up moisture. Then, tiny animals will munch away and break it up.

# How can I have a green house?

A 'green' home might have solar panels, solar collectors and a wind turbine on the roof (see pages 24–25). Insulation would be fitted to keep the heat in. Outside, rainwater would be collected in a tank, and kitchen waste put in a compost bin.

● Turn down the heating by 1°C to save energy and cut the heating bills. You won't even notice the difference.

Solar panels

Solar collectors

Compost bin

Conservatory traps heat

# When is 'off' not 'off'?

Appliances left on standby, rather than turned off, use between 10 and 60 per cent of the power they use when they are on. Turn off your television, hi-fi and computer monitor when you're not using them.

● In the UK, the average household has 12 machines on standby at any one time. That's a lot of wasted energy.

# Why are some light bulbs greedy?

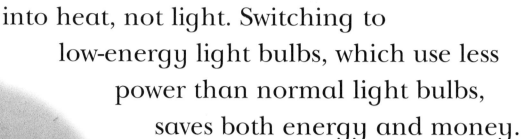

Most of the energy that goes into standard light bulbs is changed into heat, not light. Switching to low-energy light bulbs, which use less power than normal light bulbs, saves both energy and money.

Wind turbine

Rainwater tank

# How else can I save energy?

Switch lights off when you can, and try not to use too much hot water. When you have a shower or bath, or make a hot drink, use only as much water as you need.

Insulated walls

● One energy-saving light bulb uses up to a quarter of the electricity that ordinary light bulbs use, yet it will last up to 12 times longer.

# Index